hard
questions
people ask
about the
christian faith

Case Van Kempen

FAITH
ALIVE®
Christian Resources

Grand Rapids, Michigan

We thank Case Van Kempen, pastor of Maplewood Reformed Church, Holland, Michigan, for writing this book.

Faith Alive Christian Resources published by CRC Publications.
Hard Questions People Ask About the Christian Faith, © 2002 by CRC Publications, 2850 Kalamazoo Ave. SE, Grand Rapids, MI 49560. All rights reserved. With the exception of brief excerpts for review purposes, no part of this book may be reproduced in any manner whatsoever without written permission from the publisher. Printed in the United States of America on recycled paper. ✪

We welcome your comments. Call us at 1-800-333-8300 or e-mail us at editors@faithaliveresources.org.

Library of Congress Cataloging-in-Publication Data
Van Kempen, Case, 1955-
    Hard questions people ask about the Christian faith / Case Van Kempen.
        p. cm.
    ISBN 1-56212-809-4
    1. Christianity--Miscellanea. I. Title.

BR96 .V32 2001
230--dc21

                                        2001055590

10 9 8 7 6 5 4 3 2 1

For Leigh

contents

introduction

I n my parents' home, in an upstairs hallway, there's a framed photograph of a toddler sitting on the floor, playing with an old-fashioned alarm clock. You can tell this bright-eyed child, so full of curiosity, would love to take the clock apart, to literally see what makes it tick.

That's what this book is about too. We're going to sit down with a series of hard questions about the Christian faith and see if we can figure out what makes it tick. Obviously, these twelve chapters aren't going to answer every question about Christianity. But then, we don't need to know every last thing about how a clock works to trust that it's telling us the correct time either. The purpose of this book is to answer enough questions about the Christian faith to help us begin trusting that Christianity is telling us the truth.

Now, if you are anything like me, when you pick up a new book you wonder about the author's qualifications. Who is this person, and why should I believe what he has to say? I don't claim to be the supreme authority on the Christian faith; rather, I think of myself as someone who has seen a lot of clocks taken apart and put back together again.

Here's what I mean by that. For many years, my father had a second job repairing watches and clocks. He had a small workshop in our home, and on many evenings and Saturdays, he would spend hours bent over his workbench, taking apart, cleaning, repairing, and reassembling every imaginable kind of timepiece.

When I was a very young child, barely able to see the top of his workbench, I had no idea what I was looking at. Tiny screws and gears and springs lay in neatly arranged rows, but I didn't know what they were called or how they went together. If you had pointed at something and asked me its name, I probably would have said, "That's a 'Don't touch!'"

As the years went by, I kept standing by the workbench, and I began to learn the right names for all the different clock and watch parts. I began to understand how they fit together. My father could name a part or a tool, and I could hand it to him. I learned what makes a clock tick.

In the same way, I've been learning about the Christian faith. I've watched God at work in the churches that I've served; I've seen God carefully take apart, clean, repair, and reassemble people's lives. Along the way I've learned the names of a few things. I've seen how a couple of things fit together. And even though there are still countless questions to which I don't know the answers, I've learned enough to trust that the Christian faith is telling the truth about our time.

This is why I've written this book—not to answer every question, but to answer enough questions so that you too will have faith in Jesus Christ.

Case Van Kempen
Holland, Michigan

CHAPTER 1

"hello? is anybody out there?"

How can I know that God exists?

ometime during the mid-1970s, my college room-
mate and I drove to Chicago for a weekend visit.
Other than shopping and riding the elevator to the
top of the Sears Tower, we didn't have any specific plans;
we were just going to be tourists.

After spending Friday night at a friend's home, we
took a commuter train into downtown early Saturday
morning. As we walked from the station toward the

Lake Michigan waterfront, we decided that our first stop would be Chicago's famed Art Institute. Either it was still too misty to get a good view from the Sears Tower, or else we must have thought that telling our friends we had gone to Chicago to visit the Art Institute would sound more impressive than telling them we had gone to see the Sears Tower.

From a short distance away, we could see that the steps of the Art Institute were already filling up with people, and as we walked closer to the entrance, we saw why. There were signs and banners out front announcing a special exhibit by Claude Monet.

As a young college student who hadn't yet taken any art appreciation courses, I had heard Monet's name before, and I probably could have even told you that he was an Impressionist painter. But I don't think I could have told you if he was living or deceased (the latter); I couldn't name a single one of his paintings ("Is he the guy who did *Dogs Playing Poker*?"); and my idea of an impressionist was Chevy Chase on *Saturday Night Live* pretending to be President Ford.

After we bought our tickets and entered the Monet exhibit, my art education began. I was absolutely stunned; I had never seen paintings like this before. Without knowing anything about Monet's history, his inspirations, or his techniques, even I could see that he had an incredible gift. Viewed at close range, his paintings were nothing more than indistinct, blurry smudges of paint, but viewed from farther away, they became vistas and landscapes that seemed to convey a more accurate impression of reality than even a photograph could capture. I was smitten.

I can't adequately explain it, and these may sound like the foolish ramblings of someone who doesn't know enough about art to be completely jaded yet, but Monet and I struck a deal on that early Saturday morning. I think it happened when I was in the gallery with the *Water Lilies* paintings, several expansive canvases that transport the viewer to a quiet countryside on a beautiful summer afternoon. From that moment on, I knew that Monet would always speak to me through his art. For my part, I knew that I would try to learn more about him, that I was certain to tell my friends about the incredible paintings that I had seen, and that

My idea of an impressionist was Chevy Chase on Saturday Night Live pretending to be President Ford.

whenever I had the chance to see Monet's works again, I would pause to appreciate his genius.

Fast-forward fifteen years. I had finished college (I never did take that art appreciation class) and seminary, and was the pastor of a church in northern New Jersey, just outside New York City. My brother was visiting, and I was going to take him into the city to see, among other things, the Museum of Modern Art.

As we wandered through the MOMA galleries, sometimes appreciative, sometimes befuddled ("Does it look to you like that woman's head is upside down?"), we came into a room where the canvases stopped me dead in my tracks. Without so much as glancing at the identifying tags on the walls, I knew that these were works by Claude Monet. His handiwork was unmistakable, his brush strokes so distinctive as to defy imitation.

Telling you about my experiences with Monet is the best way I can think of to explain how we can know that God exists. The universe in which we live is God's canvas and our world is one of God's greatest masterpieces; the divine brush strokes are evident everywhere we look. Even before we know the Artist, we can identify the Artist's work.

Theologians call this *general revelation*. Scientists may use the term *intelligent design*. What they mean is that the creation itself reveals the hand of the Creator. Just as Monet's *Water Lilies* canvases begin to teach us about Monet, a close observation of the world around us reveals God.

Does everyone agree on this? Unfortunately, the answer is no. Many people choose not to see any evidence of a Creator's hand at work in the universe. They look for scientific explanations of how everything came to be, beginning with a Big Bang (I like to think that God said, "Bang!"), continuing through billions of years of cooling and coalescing matter, resulting in you and me. Believing in the presence of God, however, does not mean that we have to discard science or reject the self-evident history of the universe. Rather, science can become one more way in which we see the amazing evidence of God's handiwork (see chapter 8).

Others demand logical proofs for God's existence. I recall a college philosophy course in which we read at least a half-dozen authors, all of whom were trying to convince themselves of God's existence. I didn't find any of the "proofs" very persuasive. As with the scientists who see only nature at work without seeing nature's Author, anyone reading these philosophers' proofs could easily come to a non-God conclusion.

This is not to say that God isn't specifically identified in creation. *Specific revelation,* as theologians call it, is what we find when we look for the nametag next to the artwork. In God's Word, the Bible, God is identified. In it we learn something about the way God works. As with a gallery catalog at an art exhibition, some works are more fully explained than others. In the case of God's Word, most of the emphasis is on God's greatest masterpiece—redemption. (This is the masterpiece that depicts the coming of Jesus Christ into the world, his death on the cross for sinners, and his resurrection from the grave.) But even if we never look for an identification tag and never page through a catalog explaining the works of art, we can still be confident that there is one Artist behind the creation of the world and that we are part of his handiwork.

I never met Claude Monet in person, but I have no doubt that he existed, because I've seen his works. I've never seen God either—at least not in the way that we usually think of meeting an artist—but I've seen God's works too, some of which are yet to be finished. Even if I didn't know God's name, I would be convinced that some great Artist has been lovingly painting the canvas of the universe.

Questions for reflection and discussion

1. Where do you see evidence of "intelligent design" in the world around us?

2. Great artists sign their canvases. Can you find God's signature in the world? If so, where?

3. Standing very close to a painting allows us to see the artist's individual brush strokes, while standing further away gives us "the big picture." Is it easier to see evidence of God by looking closely at the world or by looking for the big picture?

4. If you could ask God to explain any part of the creation, which part would it be? Why?

5. Do you believe that your own life is the end product of nature taking its course over billions of years? Or are you the work-in-progress of a master artist?

6. What is the most compelling evidence that God exists?

CHAPTER 2

"where does God get the players for his team?"

Why would God be interested in me?

T he young mother who came to my study was obviously having problems with self-esteem. In the note she had sent, asking to meet with me, she had even signed her name with all lower-case letters, as if using any capitals would indicate a self-worth that she didn't feel.

As we talked, she began to tell me about all of the "awful" things she had done in the past, none of which sounded particularly unusual to me. I didn't try to deny or minimize her feelings, of course, but by the end of an hour together, her relentless flood of self-negativity had me ready to scream.

I know that screaming is generally considered poor form in a counselor, but I wished that she could see herself as others saw her. For example, I knew that her parents thought that she was a wonderful daughter; her husband was devoted to her; her children said she was a loving, caring mother; and even many of her friends would have given glowing testimonials about what a good friend she was to them.

At the moment, she couldn't see any of this. All she could think about were her flaws. In her discouragement, she even told me that God no longer listened to her.

Does this sound familiar? Have you ever known someone like this? Or has there ever been a time when this description would have applied to you? If so, you're not alone. The young woman I've described is actually a composite of many people, both men and women, who have come to my study over the last seventeen years. Some of them were mildly discouraged and just needed a listening ear for a few minutes. Others, more deeply in the grips of self-doubt, I referred to professional counselors. But one thing many of them shared was the question of why God would care about them when they saw so little in themselves that they considered worthy of interest.

God chooses people out of love for them, not because of their ability to do something for God.

This attitude about God reminds me of the way I used to feel in gym class when I was in grade school. Our gym teacher had the unfortunate habit of picking two students to be team captains for many games. These captains then selected the teams.

The biggest, fastest, and strongest kids were always chosen first. Then came the ones who were the friends of those already picked. Finally, after all the "worthy" children were chosen, the team captains were forced to show interest in the scrawny leftovers, which included me.

Based on what we read in God's Word, it seems pretty clear that God doesn't pick and choose people the way we do. In fact, God seems quite eager to love many people whom the world might regard as useless—misfits, outcasts, even criminals. God chooses people out of love for them, not because of their ability to do something for God.

This relationship of love is certainly one thing that sets the Christian faith apart from many other faiths. In some beliefs, the gods seem to regard humanity as little more than pawns in a celestial game of chess. In others, the primary relationship between people and the god they worship is fear. In still others, the gods need to be implored, placated, begged, or bribed to pay attention to the human supplicant.

One example of this is found in the biblical story of the prophet Elijah competing with the prophets of the more popular god, Baal, on Mount Carmel (1 Kings 18). Four hundred fifty priests of Baal were going to ask their god to send down fire; the vastly outnumbered Elijah was then going to do the same.

After more than half a day of pleading, Baal's prophets failed to arouse their god (Elijah had helpfully suggested that their god might be sleeping). When it was Elijah's turn, God responded immediately, sending a devastating fire that completely stunned all the people.

Perhaps an even more helpful story is the parable Jesus told about the unjust judge and the persistent widow, found in Luke 18. Many people think of God as a stern judge who is just waiting to find fault and dish out punishment, but Jesus gives a different picture. In the parable, a judge "who neither feared God nor cared about men" was approached by a widow who was seeking justice. At first, he refused to hear her case, but she kept coming back again and again. Finally, the judge thought to himself, "Even though I don't fear God or care about men, yet because this widow keeps bothering me, I will see that she gets justice, so that she won't eventually wear me out with her coming!" (vv. 4-5).

Now, please understand that it was not Jesus' point to say that God is like this unjust judge, only showing reluctant regard for us if we first wear him down. On the contrary, Jesus said, "And will not God bring about justice for his chosen ones, who cry out to him day and night?" (v. 7). In other words, if even this corrupt judge who cares for no one will finally give the widow what she wants, won't God, who loves the people he has chosen—his elect—respond even more quickly?

Which brings us back to the question, "But why would God 'elect' me?" What does God see in me that no one else sees? Why would he be interested in me?

We might as well go to a hospital delivery room and ask a new mother and father why they are interested in their newborn child. "Interested?" they might respond. "What kind of question is that? We love our child!" They love that child because it is theirs. They gave it life; it belongs to them, and always will.

In the same way, the God who gave each of us life loves us and cares for us. Like any parent, God longs for our love in return, but even if we sometimes fail to show that love, God doesn't stop loving us. If we sometimes fail to sense that love, it isn't because the love has stopped—it's only that something is interfering with our awareness of it.

Many times, when people have come to my study wondering whether God still loves them, I've wanted to say, "Have you murdered anyone? David did, and God kept loving him. Have you been sexually irresponsible? The woman of Samaria was, and Jesus loved her. Have you ever denied knowing Jesus? Peter did, and God kept loving him." I never said these things, at least not on a first visit, but they are true nonetheless.

You may wonder just *how much* God loves us. The Bible says that God loved the world—you and me and everybody else who will ever live on the earth—so much that "he gave [us] his one and only Son, that whoever believes in him shall not perish but have eternal life" (John 3:16). Now that's a lot of love.

Our heavenly Father is not only interested in us, he loves us immensely; and that's the greatest kind of interest there can be.

Questions for reflection and discussion

1. Why is it hard to see ourselves as others see us when we are feeling discouraged?

2. What traits do people look for when choosing someone for a job? For a sports team? As a friend?

3. Do parents withhold their love until they see if any of these traits develop in their children? Why or why not?

4. If God were interested only in "winners," who do you think would be chosen for God's team? Why? Would you want to be a part of that team?

5. Why do you think God kept loving David, the woman of Samaria, or Peter, even after they had behaved irresponsibly? How can that encourage you?

CHAPTER
3

"read any good books lately?"

Why is the Bible so hard to read?

ight now on my bedside table there are two novels, one by John Grisham, the other by Ben Bova (I have a weakness for science fiction). There are also two books of essays by humorist Dave Barry and some magazines—one Road and Track, one Sail, and four Newsweeks (I get behind). Over the next few weeks (OK, months), I know that I will read every one of these books and magazines from cover to cover. During that same period of time, I know that I am not likely to do the same with the Bible.

It's not that I don't read the Bible—I just don't read it the same way I read other kinds of material. Even the name by which we commonly refer to it tells us that it's different: it's not just the Bible, it's the Holy Bible. *Holy* means "exalted," "divine," "sacred," or "set apart," while *Bible* simply means "book"; the word comes from the ancient Phoenician city of Byblos, which exported papyrus. When we put the two words together, we get a book that is set apart from all others.

We might expect that such a book would be easy to read. We might expect that God's story would be so gripping—such a page-turner—that no one could put it down until he or she had read the last sentence. Yet this is clearly not the case. Many people who pick up the Bible, intending to read it through, get through Genesis pretty easily, slow down a bit in Exodus and Leviticus, really bog down in Numbers, and go back to reading Grisham before they ever make it to Deuteronomy. In my own Bible reading, about a chapter a day is the best I can do if I want to get anything out of it.

I suppose we could say that if the Bible were as easy to read as other books, it would also be as easily forgotten. Did you ever finish a novel and discover within a few days that you couldn't even remember the main character's name? God certainly doesn't want that to happen when we read the Bible, but that's really not an adequate explanation of why the Bible is so challenging.

Perhaps the first thing we need to be aware of is that the Bible contains many different kinds of writing. Some of it is straightforward narrative, telling the story of God's people. Other parts, like Matthew, Mark, Luke, and John, are gospels ("good news"), biographical narratives written for a particular purpose. There is poetry, (most evident in the Psalms), prophecy, law, wisdom literature (such as the book of Proverbs), letters (also referred to as epistles, many of which were written by an early missionary named Paul), and even an exotic category known as apocalyptic literature, referring to events that will take place at the end of time. These are just some of the categories, many of which can be further subdivided.

> *There is a consistency about the Bible's message that makes it easy to believe that God was guiding each of the different authors.*

Making a list like this, using words like *epistle* or *apocalyptic,* is the kind of thing that can make the Bible seem hard to read. Even the language we use to talk about the Bible can sometimes be difficult to understand. I'm no linguist, but I think some of this must date back to the Middle Ages, when ordinary people didn't read the Bible for themselves because many of them couldn't read. They trusted their priests to tell them what was in God's Word, and the priests may have wanted to shroud their work in a bit of mystery. This is pure speculation on my part, but I've noticed that the same thing is often true today. Some of the books written about the Bible make it seem as if you need a Ph.D. to understand it correctly.

You don't. It is helpful, however, to at least identify the style of writing that you are reading. We read poetry in a different way than we read history; we read letters in a different way than we read law. Knowing the type of writing will help us understand what the particular author was trying to say.

Speaking of authors, it is also good to remember that the Bible is a compilation of sixty-six different books that were written by different people over a period of thousands of years. Much of it was not even written down at first, but was handed down by recitation and memorization. Even when all of it was finally recorded in written form, it wasn't assembled into the one book we call the Bible until many years after the time of Jesus.

Most Christians believe that all of these different authors were inspired by God as they wrote their histories, prophecies, and gospels. In fact, when we consider everything that they have in common, even though separated by hundreds of years and vastly different circumstances, the similarities and connections between the sixty-six books are amazing.

For example, the Garden of Eden in Genesis has a lot in common with the future paradise that is described in the book of Revelation. The exodus of the Israelites from captivity in Egypt to the joy of the promised land teaches a great deal about God's plan for rescuing people from their sins as revealed in the four gospels. The good shepherd of Psalm 23 bears a striking resemblance to Jesus, who even calls himself the Good Shepherd. And the teachings of the Old Testament prophets are echoed in Paul's New Testament letters to the earliest churches, as they strive to become the beginning of God's new kingdom on earth.

From beginning to end, there is a consistency about the Bible's message that suggests that God was guiding each of the different authors. As a result, there's something for everyone—some people respond to poetry, others to history or parables, still others to complex theological arguments. No matter which part of the Bible we favor, God's message soon makes itself clear.

The same is also true of the different levels of complexity in God's Word. The stories of Genesis are simple enough to teach to very young children, as are many of the stories about Jesus, but I probably wouldn't try to put them to bed with one of Paul's letters or a prophecy like Ezekiel.

It is one of the miraculous blessings of the Bible that we can grow up with it and never outgrow it. It is true that parts of it may be hard to read today, but tomorrow those may be the very passages that strengthen our faith and commitment. Of one thing we can be certain: no matter which part we turn to, all of the Bible is truly God's Word.

Questions for reflection and discussion

1. Are there stories from the Bible you remember hearing as a child? What do they mean to you today?

2. Thousands of ancient biblical texts that authenticate the Bible can still be examined today. How might this help us believe that the Bible is genuine?

3. Some passages from the Bible seem to be open to more than one interpretation. Could that be intentional on God's part? Why or why not?

4. The Bible—which was written in Hebrew, Greek and a little Aramaic—has been translated into dozens of different languages and versions. Why might it be good to have many languages and versions of the Bible? What problems might this cause?

CHAPTER
4

"is there more to Easter than the Easter bunny?"

Who is Jesus Christ, and did he really rise from the dead?

When *Columbus set sail for the Far East in 1492, many people thought that the Niña, Pinta, and Santa Maria would sail right off the edge of the world, or, at the very least, be eaten by giant sea monsters. Around their borders, maps of the time were marked with the phrase "Here be dragons" (leave it to modern cartographers to take all the fun out of maps).*

As it turned out, the nay-sayers were wrong. By not sailing off the edge of the world, Columbus and his crew provided strong evidence for the theory that the world was round. It's not hard to imagine, however, that upon his return, many people still doubted the explorer. For one thing, he couldn't bring back photographs ("Oh look, here's one of first mate Sebastian standing under a banana tree"). For another, any unusual plants or animals Columbus brought back might have come from Africa. Even his log books could have been faked. Ultimately, people either had to accept the word of Columbus and his crew, or go on believing that the world was flat.

The same thing is true of our belief in Jesus. We can accept the historical record of Jesus' life and believe the testimony of eyewitnesses, along with Jesus' own testimony, or we can continue to question the validity of the evidence. There are just as many reasons to believe in the life, death, and resurrection of Jesus as there are to believe in the voyages of Columbus, and yet few people doubt whether Columbus actually sailed to the New World.

If it matters to anyone, Columbus apparently believed in Jesus; his flagship was named for Mary, Jesus' mother. Columbus lived more than five hundred years ago, which puts him that much closer to the time when Jesus lived. If we go back another five hundred years or so, (let's stretch it to seven hundred), we find the record of Emperor Charlemagne, another believer. No one seriously questions whether he lived and ruled the west from A.D. 800 to 814. Just about another four hundred years earlier, and we're to the time of Saint Augustine, Bishop of Hippo (the modern city of Bône, Algeria). Scholars accept the accounts of his life and the authenticity of his writings, in which he clearly stated that he believed in the truth of Jesus' existence. If we go back another four hundred years, we're to the time of the apostles themselves, Jesus' closest followers, most of whom lost their lives because they insisted on telling others that Jesus was exactly who he said he was.

In other words, from our modern time back to the days of Caesar Augustus (27 B.C.-A.D. 14), and Herod the Great (ca. 73-74 B.C.), there is an unbroken chain of people who have believed in the existence of Jesus of Nazareth.

The real question, as it turns out, is not whether there ever was a popular rabbi in first-century Palestine known by the name Jesus, but whether his claims about his own life are credible. Was he, as claimed to be, the Son of God? Was he born without the participation of a human father? Did he perform miracles? Did he rise from the dead after being put to death on a cross? What kind of evidence exists for these claims?

The most significant evidence would probably be some kind of proof for his most outrageous claim, that he rose from the dead. A photograph of him holding a copy of the *Jerusalem Times* printed on the Monday after his execution might convince a few doubters; so would a little DNA evidence. But since we don't have any of those things, we have to rely on the testimony of the people who saw him.

Allow me to insert a personal comment here. When I was a student at Wayne State University Law School, I spent a summer working as a bailiff in Michigan's 61st District Court. In that capacity, I got to sit in on a lot of trials and hear a lot of witnesses. It never ceased to amaze me how two or more people could witness the same event and come up with such different accounts of what happened, even when they had no reason to fabricate their own version of the story.

This is one of the things that helps me believe in the testimonies recorded in Matthew, Mark, Luke, and John: they clearly didn't scheme together in order to tell identical stories about Jesus. Each tells his own account of the events of Jesus' life, and there are just enough variations in these accounts to make them entirely credible.

More important, perhaps, is the fact that I can't see any reason for them to make up their accounts, which would mean putting their own lives at risk. The same was true later for the apostle Paul and the thousands of early believers who faced the wrath of Rome. Unless we believe that these fishermen (the previous trade of several of the disciples) were an incredibly talented group of subversive revolutionaries planning a new religion to replace Judaism and challenge the authority of Rome— and that they were willing to get themselves killed in the meantime—it's far more likely that they were witnesses simply telling their own version of what they had seen and heard.

> *A photograph of Jesus holding a copy of the Jerusalem Times printed on the Monday after his execution might convince a few doubters.*

I am convinced that this is what happened: the apostles witnessed Jesus' crucifixion and then saw him alive three days later. This caused them to go back and think about the other things they had seen and heard—

the miraculous healings, the controversial teachings, the debates with the religious professionals, and the words of prophets who had predicted these events for thousands of years. They—or someone who knew them—eventually wrote these stories down so that the truth about Jesus could be passed on to others.

Yet, in spite of the biblical record, in spite of other historical accounts, in spite of the rapid growth and spread of the early church, in spite of all the evidence that Jesus was who he claimed to be, believing in Jesus is still a matter of faith. You've got to give me credit for waiting almost four whole chapters before saying this, but there's a reason that they call it the Christian "faith." It's easy to lay out the very compelling evidence for Jesus' life, but whether anyone believes that evidence remains a matter of faith.

But then, in 1492, so was believing that the world is round.

Questions for reflection and discussion

1. Wouldn't it have made more sense for God's Son to make a dramatic appearance in Rome, the capital of the empire, rather than being born as an infant to poor parents in a far-flung province?

2. Why do you think so little is known about the life of Jesus before he began his public ministry at about age thirty? How would Jesus' life on earth have been different if people had always known him to be the Son of God?

3. Early in his ministry, Jesus often told the people whom he cured of illnesses not to tell anyone what had happened. Why do you think Jesus wanted them to stay quiet?

4. After his resurrection, as he was about to return to his Father in heaven, Jesus sent his disciples to be his witnesses in every part of the earth. Why did Jesus want his followers to be his witnesses, rather than staying on earth himself to tell others?

5. Which seems more persuasive to you: (a) historical evidence for the life, death, and resurrection of Jesus; (b) the influence Jesus has had on the history of the world; or (c) the personal testimonies of people who claim that Jesus is making a difference in their lives today?

CHAPTER
5

"going up . . . or down?"

Would a loving God allow anyone to go to hell?

The wedding was scheduled for 4:00 p.m. By 10:00 a.m., our small country church had been beautifully decorated with flowers and candles; by noon, the food for the reception was cooking in the kitchen; by 3:30 p.m., the guests were beginning to arrive. Everyone was in a festive mood—except the bride and groom. One of their most important guests, the maid of honor, had not yet arrived.

Setting aside any superstitions about seeing each other before the ceremony, the bridal couple came to find me in my study. I looked up from my notes, surprised to see them looking so distressed. When they told me about the missing maid of honor, I asked a few questions: Did they know where she was getting ready for the wedding? Had anyone called to see if she was on her way? Had anyone gone to look for her?

Before they could answer, one of the groom's attendants burst into the room and breathlessly announced that the missing girl had been in a car accident and was being taken by ambulance to a city hospital about an hour away. He reported that she had a broken arm and that she had suffered other bruises and lacerations, but none of her injuries appeared to be life-threatening.

Within moments, as news of the accident spread through the church, we were joined by the other members of the wedding party. As we talked, a picture of what had happened earlier in the afternoon began to develop. Several of the attendants and their friends—but not the bride and groom—had been at the maid of honor's home, celebrating in advance of the wedding. A significant amount of alcohol had been consumed. When the maid of honor finally left home to drive to the church, she missed a stop sign, drove straight through an intersection, and plowed into the ditch.

As concerned as everyone was for the injured woman, the immediate question was whether or not to proceed with the wedding. The church was decorated, the food was ready, and the guests were waiting. When the bride and groom asked me what I thought, I said, "It's up to you, of course, but if you think the maid of honor feels bad now, imagine how she's going to feel when she sobers up and hears that you canceled the ceremony on her account." After a few more minutes of discussion— and some quick changes in the order of the remaining attendants—we proceeded with the ceremony.

It's not by chance that God's Word so often compares heaven to a bridal celebration. Invitations have been sent out, the wedding feast is being prepared, guests are already beginning to assemble. The only thing we don't know for sure is the appointed time. Although we've been given some signs to tell us when that time is near, all we know for certain is that God wants us to be ready when the bridegroom, Jesus, appears, to be joined with his bride, the Church, for all eternity.

When we look at the promise of heaven in this way, it seems fairly clear that the invited guests have the freedom to choose whether or not they will be present for the ceremony and the eternal celebration that will follow. It isn't that they haven't been invited, and it isn't that God doesn't want them to be there; rather, they may choose, for a variety of reasons, not to respond to the invitation.

In Matthew 22, Jesus tells of a king who gave a wedding feast for his son. When he sent his servants to call those who were invited, some flatly refused to come. Others made light of the invitation, and went off to tend to their farms or businesses. The king then told his servants to bring in anyone they could find—anyone at all—until the wedding hall was finally filled.

This part of the story seems to say that God's invitation is for anyone who will respond. The story pointedly says that those who finally accepted the invitation included "both good and bad"; in other words, there was no distinction made between worthy and unworthy guests. People were free to make their own decision about attending.

Yet, as the story continues, when the king went to see all those who had come to the feast, he found a man who wasn't wearing a proper wedding garment. The king had him thrown out "into the darkness, where there will be weeping and gnashing of teeth." This part

A wedding invitation should begin to make a difference in the way we live and in the choices we make.

of the story certainly makes it seem as if God does consign people to hell.

The same seems to be true in another wedding parable, in which ten maidens were waiting for a bridegroom to appear at night. The story in Matthew 25 tells us that five of the maidens had prepared their lamps and brought extra oil, while five others had been foolish and ran out of oil. When the bridegroom appeared, the five foolish maidens had gone in search of more oil. By the time they arrived at the wedding feast—which they seemed eager to attend, had it not been for their lack of oil—the door was already closed and they were left outside in the dark.

Can we say that a loving God is sending improperly clothed guests and foolish maidens to hell? Or would it be more accurate to say that the garment-less wedding guest and five of the maidens chose not to let the king's invitation make any difference in their lives? If we understand the wedding garment and the oil to be symbols of faith, who has really made the choice to be left out of the wedding feast?

As the foolish maid of honor at my country wedding painfully learned, a wedding invitation should begin to make a difference in the way we live and in the choices we make. The wedding day, of all days, was not the day to be drinking and driving. By her own foolish choices, the maid of honor missed the ceremony.

In the same way, having been invited to the eternal wedding feast for God's Son, we are being given time to prepare for that day by faith—and even faith is a free gift. The custom in Jesus' day was that the host of the wedding handed out the wedding garments. All the guests had to do was put them on!

Again and again in God's Word, we discover how patient God is being with the invited guests, giving them every opportunity to respond. We see how generous is the gift of faith, and how God makes no distinction between worthy or unworthy guests. After all this, if the guests still choose not to respond to God's invitation, can we really say that it is God who is sending people to hell?

This answer doesn't address people who have never heard the gospel invitation, nor does it say anything about those who may have heard it incorrectly. Again, the consistent message of God's Word is mercy and grace. I believe we can trust that God will not unfairly exclude anyone from the wedding feast of his Son.

It does seem to be clear, however, that accepting God's invitation is a choice we make for ourselves. If we are truly determined to miss the wedding, God will not force us to come.

Questions for reflection and discussion

1. What are some of the ways in which heaven is like a wedding?

2. What are some of the ways in which we prepare to attend a wedding? How do these compare with the ways in which living by faith prepares us for heaven?

3. Why do you think God hasn't told us the exact day and time of Jesus' return to earth?

4. What are some of the reasons that people reject God's free gift of faith in Jesus Christ? If they've "thrown away the invitation," so to speak, will God give them another one? How many times?

5. Once the wedding feast begins, the Bible says that the door is closed. Wouldn't a loving God open the door just one more time for the people who really wanted to get in? What do you think?

"they're different bags, but the same groceries, right?"

Don't sincere people of all faiths actually worship the same God?

Driving through the countryside on my way to an appointment in the city, I saw something that I could hardly believe. There, sitting alongside a gravel farm driveway, was a screaming red Ferrari—and it had a "for sale" sign on it!

Now, just in case you are the kind of practical person who thinks that a car is nothing more than a transportation appliance, something to reliably get you from point A to point B, you should know that a Ferrari is an outrageously expensive, limited-production, high performance Italian sports car. General Motors builds more cars in one day than Ferrari builds in an entire year, and you could easily buy four or five of GM's finest vehicles for the price of a single Ferrari.

This is why I found it so hard to believe that some farmer had a Ferrari sitting in his driveway. I know that many farmers appreciate fine machinery, but it tends to be of the green, John Deere variety. You don't see a lot of farmers going to the feed mill in Italian two-seaters.

I needed to get to my appointment, so I didn't have time to stop and take a closer look at the car, but I made a mental note as to the location of the farm, and decided that if the car was still there, I would investigate this mystery on my way home.

Later that afternoon, I pulled into the farm driveway, shaking my head in disbelief. There it was in all its Ferrari-red glory: the classic five-spoke wheels, the Prancing Horse badges, the Pontiac Fiero interior, the . . . wait a minute. Pontiac Fiero? Sure enough, upon closer inspection, the car turned out to be an imitation. Someone had bolted a replica Ferrari body onto a Pontiac chassis. From a short distance away, it was a convincing illusion, but up close, it was clearly not the real thing.

I'm sure the imitation Ferrari would have worked just fine to get the driver from point A to point B, but that didn't make it a Ferrari. Having other people "oooh" and "aaah" over it wouldn't make it a Ferrari. If some unsuspecting buyer purchased the car, believing that it was the real thing, that still wouldn't make it a Ferrari. Nothing you could do to this car would get you in the door at the Ferrari Owner's Club. For all its gorgeous looks, it simply wasn't a Ferrari.

This is the problem with every world religion other than Christianity. It may sound phenomenally arrogant to say this, and I'll be the first to acknowledge that it's not a very popular position today, but here goes anyway: every other religion is a fake. They may perform some of the same functions as Christianity, they may attract large crowds of sincere believers, they may even have a very satisfying allure, but there is only one way to salvation, and that is through Jesus Christ.

The only thing that makes this statement tolerable is the fact that God is giving away Ferraris. By that I mean to say that God is offering the real thing—eternal life—as a free gift to anyone who wants it. While many other religions place huge "ownership" demands on their adherents, faith in Jesus Christ is free. There is no purchase price, no qualifying test, no membership fee. When people believe the claims of Christianity, all they have to do is receive it. God is giving it away for free.

I hope you will believe me when I say that I know this issue is much more complicated than this. I know that faith is not a Ferrari; I know that heaven is not a Ferrari Owner's Club. But I do find it helpful to strip arguments down to their most basic components, and then keep those simple truths in mind as I examine the more complicated elements of the issue under consideration.

So, for example, in this question of the validity of other religions, the complicating challenge that nearly stops me in my tracks every time is the kind of statement a wise, elderly gentleman once said to me, "I fully accept that if I had been born in a Muslim country to a Muslim family, I would be a Muslim today."

Should we accept that faith is an accident of birth, and should this lead us to believe that any religion is acceptable, as long as the believer is sincere about it? That's the statement I so often hear: "It doesn't really matter what you are, as long as you're a good one."

The Bible certainly doesn't support this position. Jesus said, "No one comes to the Father except through me" (John 14:6b), and the apostle Paul didn't teach that you can just keep on believing whatever you want to . believe, as long as you are sincere about it.

What Paul noticed about the people of Athens (Acts 17) was that they were inclined to be religious—so much so, in fact, that they had erected an altar in their city with the inscription, "To an unknown God." They were covering all the bases—if some unknown deity had done them any favors, they wanted to make sure that he or she was properly honored. Paul told them that there was only one true God worthy of their honor, and that this God had sent a Savior, whom he had raised from the dead. By presenting them with the truth, Paul hoped to turn the Athenians away from the worship of their numerous false gods.

God is offering the real thing—eternal life—as a free gift to anyone who wants it.

Today, the presentation of the gospel, the good news about the one God of heaven and earth and his Son, Jesus, can still convince people that even the religion of their childhood may fall short of the truth. Their desire to be religious is a good thing, but it may have been misdirected. When they examine the claims of the Bible alongside their own faith and the other religions of the world, it becomes apparent that only God's Word is the real thing.

Let's go back to the Ferrari for a moment. Imagine that you, like me, had been born with an inclination to love cars, but all you had ever seen were Chevys. Then imagine that someone brought a Ferrari to your door. Would you be able to tell the difference?

Through the work of the Holy Spirit, God has created within us a longing for spiritual truths. When we take a close look at all the claims of Christianity, we will discover that faith in Jesus alone is the "real thing," the only way to eternal life.

And God is giving it away for free.

Questions for reflection and discussion

1. If you had been raised in a culture in which Christianity was not the dominant religion (which may well describe you), do you think you ever would have seriously considered the claims of Christianity?

2. In what ways might other religions prepare people for faith in Jesus Christ?

3. Why do you think some countries prohibit the teaching of Christianity? Why are they unwilling to let people hear about the Christian faith?

4. If we accepted the statement "It doesn't matter what you are as long as you're a good one," what difference would that make in the way we live?

5. In the Ten Commandments (Exodus 20) God describes himself as "a jealous God." What do you think this means? How would the history of the world have been different if people had worshiped only the one true God?

"do we really need a church on every corner?"

Why are there so many churches? Which one is right?

W hen I lived in western New York, the church where I was pastor was part of a regional association of churches that covered a wide geographical area. So four times a year, one of the elders of my church and I would get up before dawn and drive several hours to whichever church was hosting our quarterly meeting.

One of those churches was located in Palmyra, New York, the place where the Mormon Church began (known today as the Church of Jesus Christ of Latter Day Saints). Every time we drove there, we would pass by a large golden statue of the angel Moroni. According to Mormon doctrine, it was Moroni who appeared to Joseph Smith early in the nineteenth century, granting him a divine revelation out of which Mormonism was born.

One of the elders with whom I occasionally attended these meetings was a farmer who strongly disliked this statue of Moroni, which he considered as evil as any false idol from the days of the Old Testament. On one particularly bright spring day, when the early morning sun was glinting off the statue, I heard him mutter to himself, "I wonder how big a tractor and how much chain I would need to pull that statue down?" We then drove into the city of Palmyra itself, passing through an intersection where there were four different Christian churches—literally, a church on every corner.

It occurred to me on one of these trips that if anyone were ever going to persuade a follower of Joseph Smith to reject Mormonism and attend a traditional Christian church, he or she would have to be ready to explain why there were four churches at this intersection—each associated with a different Christian denomination—rather than just one. If the Christians of Palmyra couldn't agree with each other on a single church, why should any of their claims be considered more trustworthy than those of Joseph Smith?

It wasn't always this way. There was a time when there was only one body of Christian believers, a truly "catholic" church. Unfortunately, it didn't last much beyond the original twelve disciples. By the time the apostle Paul was writing to the Christians in Corinth around the middle of the first century, different factions of believers had already begun to develop. There was one group that followed Paul and another that followed the teachings of an evangelist named Apollos. Some were devoting themselves to the teachings of Cephas, while still others simply said they belonged to Christ.

Having a different church on every corner may be God's way of allowing us to reach more people with the good news of salvation.

Addressing this situation, Paul wrote, "Is Christ divided? Was Paul crucified for you? Were you baptized into the name of Paul?" (1 Corinthians 1:13). Although in name there may have been only one dominant

Christian church for many years, based first in Jerusalem and then in Rome, in reality, factions were a part of the church from its very beginning.

For this reason, the early Christians began to write creeds. A creed is a distillation of beliefs, a summary statement of faith to which everyone can give their agreement. One of the earliest is a statement about Jesus' resurrection found near the end of Paul's first letter to those same quarreling believers in Corinth: "For what I received I passed on to you as of first importance: that Jesus Christ died for our sins according to the Scriptures, that he was buried, that he was raised on the third day according to the Scriptures, and that he appeared to Peter, and then to the Twelve" (1 Corinthians 15:3-5).

A more comprehensive statement of faith is found in the Apostles' Creed, whose origins can be traced back to the second century (although some believe that it may be even older, hence the name). Beginning with God the Father, continuing with Jesus, and ending with statements about the Holy Spirit, the Church, and eternal life, it summarizes the key beliefs of the Christian faith in just slightly more than one hundred words.

Although there continued to be disputes over many of the particulars of the Christian faith during the first millennium, most believers still thought of themselves as belonging to a single church, the Church of Rome. In A.D. 1054, the Eastern Orthodox Church, based in Constantinople, rejected the authority of Rome, forming the first major division between groups of Christians. It should be noted, however, that in spite of the split, the Eastern churches still adhered to nearly all of the same key Christian beliefs that were accepted by the Church of Rome.

Another major division in the church occurred during the Protestant Reformation of the sixteenth century. What began as a desire to reform some of the specific practices of the Roman Church gave birth to many separate "protesting" churches. Many of these developed into new Christian denominations, known by the familiar titles of Lutheran, Presbyterian, Methodist, and so on. Again, nearly all of these churches still agreed with the same basic creedal statements that were accepted by the Church of Rome.

Five hundred years later, the situation is largely unchanged. The past hundred years have seen several new denominations that emphasize the work of the Holy Spirit, and there has been a more recent rise in the number of nondenominational churches. But as with each earlier division in the church, nearly all of these different bodies of believers still hold to the same core beliefs that are spelled out in the Apostles' Creed.

So why do we still find a church on every corner in Palmyra, New York?

Not surprisingly, it is the noncore beliefs that generally cause Christians to form their separate associations. For example, the language used in the worship service may be a point of contention. When Rome dictated that all worship would be in Latin, this was not an issue, but when people began to migrate to other parts of the world—and began to worship in their own languages—language and ethic background were important factors in denominational identity.

Another issue for many churches over the years has been music. At one time, the dispute was between using only what was found in the Bible (such as the Psalms) versus "man-made" music (such as hymns). Today, many churches define themselves in terms of contemporary (guitars, keyboards, drums) versus traditional (organ) music.

Doctrinal issues have also been the rallying cry for many denominations and congregations. Baptism (infant or adult), issues relating to the Lord's Supper, choice of schools (Christian or secular), the role of women in the church—all have become identifying characteristics.

In spite of all these differences on the particulars, nearly every Christian church around the world still agrees on the same essential core beliefs: God created heaven and earth; God sent Jesus Christ, his Son, to die for our sins and to be raised from the dead; and God is still active today through the Holy Spirit.

Having a different church on every corner may be perceived as a sign of our sinfulness, a visible reminder that we live in a world in which our sins cause us to think that we're right and the other guy is wrong. But it may also be God's way of allowing us to reach more people with the good news of salvation.

What is truly amazing—and a sign of God's grace— is not that we've formed so many different churches, but that after two millennia, we continue to agree on the essentials of what it means to be Christian.

Questions for reflection and discussion

1. What are some of the factors that cause people to divide into separate groups?

2. Of the different denominations you know something about, which one comes closest to matching your understanding of how to live the Christian faith? Why?

3. If you were new in town and saw a church on every corner, how would you decide which one to visit? Which one to join? Which characteristics would be most important to you?

4. Many of the church's creeds are hundreds of years old, and so in recent years some churches have written new creeds. Do you think this is a good idea? Why or why not?

5. Is it important for a church to belong to a denomination? What are some of the strengths and dangers of being an independent congregation?

"how many tyrannosaurs does it take to wreck a Garden of Eden?"

Does science contradict or disprove the Christian faith?

D o you remember Sinclair gas stations? Do you remember the big, green, inflatable dinosaurs that they used to give away? When I was in grade school, I would have given anything to bring one of those to show-and-tell.

You see, as nearly as I could tell, dinosaurs didn't exist at my Christian elementary school. They didn't exist at my church, either. I saw them everywhere else—on cereal boxes, in books, at the toy department, on "The Flintstones"—but I never heard a thing about them at school or church.

I loved dinosaurs, and to my childish mind, there wasn't any problem reconciling the story of creation in the Bible with the fossil record. Apparently, I must have been paying attention in church one time when the minister read 2 Peter 3:8: "But do not forget this one thing, dear friends: With the Lord a day is like a thousand years, and a thousand years are like a day." As far as I was concerned, that settled it. Dinosaurs could have existed on day five of creation, or even early on day six, long before God ever created Adam.

Unfortunately, many of my early teachers didn't see it that way, teaching a literal seven-day creation. They never came right out and said it, at least not that I can remember, but the clear implication was that every archeologist, every paleontologist, every zoologist—in fact, nearly every scientist studying the natural world—must be wrong. If the Bible said one thing and the entire weight of scientific evidence said another, the Bible won every time.

This insistence on reading the Bible as a contrary-to-science textbook has probably done more harm to Christian credibility than any other contemporary issue. Late-night comedians have a field day every time a state legislature debates whether the biblical account of creation should be taught alongside—or even instead of—scientific theories of how things came to be. Not just the creation stories, but every part of the biblical witness suffers by association. No dinosaurs, evidence of which I can see with my own eyes? Then how am I supposed to believe in a resurrection, which I can't see?

It wasn't until I entered seminary that I finally heard someone address this issue in a way that made sense. A professor of the Old Testament told our class that the Bible is infallible "in everything that it intends to teach." In other words, when God told Job about laying the cornerstone of the world, it wasn't intended as a scientific lesson about how the earth was made; rather, it was clearly intended as poetic imagery about sovereignty (Job 38:6). When Matthew, Mark, Luke, and

If the Bible said one thing and the entire weight of scientific evidence said another, the Bible won every time.

John disagree on some of the details of Jesus' life, we have to remember that their accounts weren't written the way modern authors write historical biographies of famous figures. These are gospels, a special kind of writing intended to convey the good news of Jesus' life, death, and resurrection. When we read the book of Revelation, pen and calendar in hand, ready to check off end-of-the-world events as they occur, we have to remember that this wasn't intended to be an itinerary for the apocalypse. Revelation was intended to comfort the victims of oppression and injustice in every age of the church.

The danger, of course, in saying that the Bible is infallible only in what it intends to teach is that readers may supply their own understanding of "intent." People who prefer to read the Bible literally are quick to point out that any biblical passage, no matter how clearly stated, can be challenged with a statement like, "Well, maybe that's not what the author intended." Nothing is certain, the literalists allege; everything is open to the question of what the author intended to teach.

But this is only true if we throw all common sense out of the window. For example, one of the Ten Commandments says, "Thou shalt not commit adultery," and many other verses in the Old Testament spell out what this means. Jesus further helped us to understand this commandment when he said, "But I tell you that anyone who looks at a woman lustfully has already committed adultery with her in his heart" (Matthew 5:28). It would take an absurdly tortured, willful misreading of the author's intent to miss the clear meaning of the seventh commandment. Does it apply to cable TV? DVDs? The Internet? Of course it does, even though these things didn't exist when the commandment was given. The intent—fidelity in relationships—is perfectly clear.

Getting back to the more specific question of the relationship between science and the Bible, it seems as if continuing scientific discoveries can actually help to strengthen our faith in God's Word. Regarding the creation accounts, scientists have long noticed how there were periods in the earth's history when things seemed to stay the same for extended periods of time, followed by rapid change, then another long period of stability. Could these be the "days" of creation?

Other researchers, peering into the farthest reaches of the universe, or into the interior of atomic particles, have spoken of intelligent design. Whether they are looking through the Hubble telescope or an electron microscope, they see the handwriting of God. Countless scientists have become people of faith, as they find no contradiction between their science and their faith.

There are some things in the Bible, of course, that will always defy scientific explanations. Miracles, by definition, appear to operate outside the natural laws of the universe (it may also be that we simply don't know all the laws!). The death and resurrection of Jesus is the greatest of these unexplained mysteries; it's a unique event that we cannot analyze scientifically by duplicating in the lab.

To believe such wonders requires faith. It doesn't mean that science is wrong; it doesn't mean that Christians have to suspend all scientific inquiry. It simply means that science cannot explain everything that we accept by faith.

Perhaps this in itself is evidence of God's hand at work in our world. Just as a big, green Sinclair dinosaur proved to a child that dinosaurs once existed—no matter what the teacher said—so a risen Savior making a difference in our lives proves that the resurrection really took place, no matter what scientists may say.

Did dinosaurs exist? Of course they did. It would be absurd to disregard the evidence right in front of our eyes. Was there a resurrection? Of course there was. It would be just as absurd to throw out the evidence of hundreds of witnesses and of our hearts.

Questions for reflection and discussion

1. Which were you taught in school: A literal seven-day creation or scientific theories about the origins of the universe? Which would you want your children to learn? Why do you think this continues to be such a sensitive subject for many people?

2. If a modern researcher proved that it was possible to stay alive for three days in the belly of a big fish, would that make the story of Jonah more believable to you? Why or why not?

3. Do you see evidence of "intelligent design" in the world? Do you believe that the universe could have evolved into its present form without any assistance from an intelligent Creator?

4. If they aren't intended to be read as scientific explanations, what lessons do the creation accounts in Genesis intend to teach us?

5. Why didn't God give us more scientifically accurate information in the Bible? Would this information have been useful to people a thousand years ago? A thousand years from now?

CHAPTER
9

"why does 'Christian' seem like a four–letter word?"

What about all the pain that has been caused in the name of Christianity?

One of the most interesting seminars I ever attended included a presentation about people who had once been actively involved in a local church, but now chose to stay far away from the fellowship of God's people. The presenter had decided that he would not try to change the minds of these church dropouts as he

traveled around the country, interviewing them. He would
simply set up his tape recorder and let them talk.

Boy, did they talk.

As we listened to some of their stories, it became
chillingly clear that the church has amazing power over
people's lives; not only the power to bring about posi-
tive changes, but also the power to inflict pain. People
care deeply about their faith, and strong emotions can
quickly come to the surface when there is a conflict
with the church.

One young woman told of her experience after her
mother died. This mother had been one of those actively
involved church members for whom God's work came
ahead of everything else. When she passed away, her
daughter wanted to give the church a generous gift in
her mother's memory. The church refused the gift. Why?
The daughter was divorced and remarried, and this con-
servative church would not accept a gift from someone
whom they considered to be living in sin.

As far as inflicting pain goes, this might seem like a
minor example; the church has certainly been guilty of
causing far greater suffering, sometimes to entire conti-
nents of people (think of how many churches once
approved of slavery). Yet even this small incident helps us

> *She was furious, and gave me an earful of everything that had ever displeased her about our church.*

to identify the main reason behind much of the pain that has been caused by the church.

In a word, that reason is judgment. I actually prefer the alternative spelling, "judgement," because it reminds us even more clearly that the church has often been guilty of setting itself up as a judge, passing sentence on the lives of the people who come under its scrutiny.

In the seemingly minor case of the woman whose memorial gift was deemed unacceptable, the church had judged that the woman's divorce and remarriage caused her to be an unrepentant sinner. They may have hoped that their harsh stance would in some way cause her to take stock of her life and mend her ways (another divorce?) before it was too late. In reality, all it did was inflict needless pain.

At the other extreme is the pain caused by many churches during the time of slavery, when people from Africa were judged to be inferior to people from Europe. Some even questioned whether the slaves had souls. Others judged that the Africans had been guilty of savagery, and that bringing them to America was actually to their benefit. Here they could learn about the God of the Bible—who, after all, told slaves to be obedient to their masters, even if they should become fellow believers (1 Timothy 6:1-2).

Passages such as this, as well as texts about women, warfare, or wealth—to name just three things—have been lifted from the context of the time and place in which they were written, and have been used to justify all kinds of judgmental behavior. Yes, the apostle Paul said that a woman should be subject to her husband, this at a time when a woman had no more rights than a table lamp. But Paul also said that husbands should love their wives as Christ loved the church—a truly radical elevation of the status of women (Ephesians 5:21ff.).

The Crusaders of the Middle Ages no doubt loved to hear about the wars of the Old Testament, justifying their own murderous campaigns to recapture Palestine from the infidels. Unfortunately, they neglected God's New Testament injunction, "Do not take revenge, my friends, but leave room for God's wrath, for it is written: 'It is mine to avenge; I will repay,' says the Lord" (Romans 12:19).

As for wealth, there is no shortage of verses that, when lifted out of context, can be used to justify the accumulation of vast fortunes, to the neglect of the poor. For example, "The wealth of the rich is their fortified city; but poverty is the ruin of the poor" (Proverbs 10:15). Once again, it takes a trip to the other Testament to find "No one can serve two masters . . . you cannot serve both God and Money" (Matthew 6:24).

If a person—or even an entire church—is inclined to be judgmental toward others, they will be able to find Scripture passages that support their behavior. But if we make an effort to understand the full counsel of God's Word, studying passages in context, and looking at related texts as well, we will find that there is never an excuse for judgmental behavior by the church. It was never God's desire that the church, or its individual members, inflict such needless pain.

Having said that, it is also important to remember that a great deal of the pain for which people assign blame to the church is actually pain that they have brought upon themselves. For example, I once received an irate long-distance phone call from an inactive member of one of the congregations I pastored. This woman had moved far away from our church, and hadn't been back for so much as a visit in more than five years. After several letters, in which I encouraged her to join a church near her new home—letters to which I received no response—the elders of my church finally decided to remove her name from our membership list.

She was furious, and gave me an earful of everything that had ever displeased her about our church—which turned out to be quite a bit, actually. But love us or hate us, she still thought of our congregation as her church, and to be told that she was no longer considered a member was very painful.

We didn't intend to cause pain, even though that was the result. We honestly thought that the woman didn't care, since she never responded to our inquiries. I suppose it could be argued that we weren't sensitive enough to her feelings, but perhaps in this case, the woman was responsible for her own pain.

As has often been said of marriage, the person who loves us best can also be the source of our greatest pain. Like an errant spouse, when the church acts in ways that are judgmental, it can hurt the very people it most wants to love and serve; and those same people can bring about their own pain when they refuse the church's love.

Questions for reflection and discussion

1. Why do you think Christians so often seem to pass judgment on other people?

2. When it comes to their relationship with God and the church, what are some of the ways in which people might cause their own pain?

3. The apostle Paul complained of a "thorn" in his side that God would not remove. What are some of the ways in which pain can be for our benefit?

4. Christians are often accused of hypocrisy—saying one thing but doing another. What are some examples of how hypocrisy can cause pain?

5. It's easy to look back in history and find fault with the church's actions during the Crusades, the era of slavery, or the Holocaust. Can you think of any current world situations in which the church is causing pain, through its activity, inactivity, or its silence?

CHAPTER
10

"why does it hurt when I laugh . . . or cry?"

How can a loving God permit so much evil in the world?

S eventh grade is an awkward year for any kid. Grade school is over, so there's a sense of having outgrown childish things, but the almost-adult status of high school is still a couple of years away. Some junior high children mature faster than others—I can remember a few of the boys in my class who looked like they needed a shave— but it was the girls especially who seemed to be more *interesting than they had been the previous year (why, exactly, was it again that we thought they had cooties?).*

My own seventh grade experience was complicated by the fact that I had changed school systems. When I nervously entered my assigned classroom on the first day (wearing my new brown corduroy pants and a striped yellow shirt), I didn't know a single kid in the room. Nearly everyone else was getting reacquainted with old friends, talking about their summer vacations. I even heard a few students saying, "Remember when . . . ?" and laughing about some common grade school experience.

I took a seat near the middle of the room and was relieved when the teacher finally introduced herself and began to talk about junior high school expectations. We then went around the room and introduced ourselves. When it was my turn, I felt so out of place that I almost expected someone to say, "Hey, are you sure you're supposed to be here?"

After a few days, I noticed another student in my class who seemed to keep to himself almost as much as I did. Jim was just about my same size and seemed to be pretty smart, but he had an odd habit of waving his hand near his mouth whenever anyone talked to him. I sat down near him in the cafeteria one day and was surprised to see that he had a whole package of lunch meat in front of him, which he was eating, slice by slice (I never got more than one meager slice per sandwich).

I mumbled some sort of greeting and opened up my own lunch bag, and pretty soon Jim and I were talking. We always sat together in the cafeteria after that, and after a few weeks, I finally asked Jim why he got so much meat in his lunch.

Nothing escapes God's notice, not even the sparrow that falls from its nest—a rather minor tragedy, as tragedies go.

"I'm supposed to eat a lot of protein," he said. He paused a moment, as if he were trying to decide whether to say anything else. Then he blurted out, "I've got cystic fibrosis." I thought he had said something about his sister, but I didn't say anything.

We kept eating, and after a few moments, Jim started to tell me a little more about his condition. He told me about his special diet, that he took a handful of pills every day, and that he wasn't supposed to catch colds. For him, a cold almost certainly meant pneumonia, which was how his habit of waving his hand had begun (he was trying to chase away germs). I learned that he slept in an oxygen tent every night and that he had to be pounded on his back twice a day to loosen up the congestion in his lungs.

Jim and I became best friends that year. We hung out together after school, we talked on the phone, we discussed girls—endlessly and hypothetically—we went to the mall, we went to the movies. I stayed over at his house a few times, sleeping on a cot next to his tent. He even got permission to stay over at my house once (we had to run a special humidifier all night long). I began to catch myself waving my hand near my mouth whenever I heard anyone cough or sneeze.

Toward the end of seventh grade, Jim seemed a little less interested in spending time together. We didn't talk as often, and by the beginning of summer vacation, I wasn't sure if I would see Jim until the fall.

Not long after the end of that school year, my mother received a phone call. When she hung up the phone, she told me that Jim was in the hospital. It was serious, she said. Would I like to go see him? We went there, found his room, and walked in. I thought I was going to be strong and brave for Jim's sake, but when I saw him lying in his hospital bed with IV tubes in his arms, I began to get sick to my stomach. I spent most of the visit in his bathroom, trying not to lose my lunch.

I probably couldn't have explained it at the time, but I was angry. Angry at Jim for having a potentially fatal disease, angry at the disease itself, angry at God. A few weeks later, when my mother gently handed me Jim's obituary notice in the paper, I told her that I didn't want to go to the visitation or the funeral. I didn't care, I said. The truth was that I didn't understand. I didn't know how to make sense out of this senseless death.

How could a loving God allow such a terrible disease to exist? Since seventh grade, I've heard that same question asked in dozens of different ways: How could God allow (pick one) wars, accidents, crime, natural disasters, illness, injustice, or cruelty of any kind—even sin itself—to exist? Why didn't God just snap his fingers and do away with evil?

Far from being silent on the subject, God's Word offers many answers to these questions. Even though they may not seem very satisfying when we are in the middle of a painful situation, they all seem to say the same thing: Trust that God knows what he is doing.

Wars? God uses them to save people—or to teach them to return to God. Illness? It often reveals a hidden faith. Injustice? It gives God's people a chance to show that there's a different way to live (not that they always choose to go that route). Natural disasters? They reveal

God's power—and humanity's pride (perhaps we shouldn't build houses on the slopes of volcanoes or on barrier islands). Even sin itself, though defeated on the cross, has been allowed to continue for a time so that those who believe in Jesus have time to persuade other sinners (and I mean that as lovingly as possible, since I'm one too) to come to the same saving faith in Jesus.

Some have suggested that evil exists because God is not completely in control of the world. God's Word assures us that just the opposite is true. Nothing escapes God's notice, not even the sparrow that falls from its nest—a rather minor tragedy, as tragedies go.

In fact, the passage in Matthew 10 about the sparrows may be God's best statement on the problem of evil. Jesus was sending his disciples out into the world on their own. He warned them about the many difficulties they would face, and assured them that his Father knew all about them. He told them about the sparrows, and then he said, "So don't be afraid; you are worth more than many sparrows."

"Don't be afraid." Obviously, this isn't the final answer to the problem of evil in the world, but for me, it is a working answer. No matter what the situation, I can trust that God is fully in control of it.

Can I tell you why my friend Jim died at such a young age? Not yet. But I know that God loved Jim, and I know that I will see him again someday.

Questions for reflection and discussion

1. What are some specific examples of evil in the world that trouble you? Can you think of any instances in which God has used an evil situation to bring about something good?

2. Does it sometimes seem to you as if God is not fully in control? Why isn't God's activity more obvious? Or do we fail to see it?

3. The Bible teaches that evil entered the world when Adam and Eve disobeyed God in the Garden of Eden. If God had simply decided to eliminate all sin, making obedience unnecessary, how would people demonstrate their love for God?

4. Have you ever heard someone who is gravely ill say, "I don't know how I could get through this without faith"? What do they mean by that? Does that same attitude help us survive other situations of evil's influence in the world?

5. The Bible says that all evil will end when Jesus returns. What are we supposed to do about it until then? What effect might this have on people who do not place their trust in God?

"does God really know what I'm worried about?"

Is Christianity relevant to my life?

O ne of the nicest birthday gifts I ever received was my very own copy of Chapman Piloting: Seamanship & Boat Handling. At 656 pages—in large format—Chapman is a big book, one that is often referred to as the Bible for sailors. Unfortunately, as is often true of the real Bible, not many sailors read their Chapman from cover to cover.

I, on the other hand, am one of those strange people who will actually read the instruction manual before plugging in the latest electronic gadget. In the same way, before I ever untied a dock line on our first sailboat, I read *Chapman* all the way through—twice. I first read a copy that I had checked out of the library, then I read the one I received for my birthday. After that, I read nearly every other book on sailing that I could find.

Some parts of these books were clearly not relevant to the kind of boating my family and I would be doing, but I read those sections anyway. For example, I read about trailer sailing (our boat would be in a slip), about tides and currents (the Great Lakes don't have much of either), and about how to right a small daysailer after capsizing (the boat we were considering weighed 12,000 pounds; I didn't think that standing on the keel was going to do much good).

Not long after I finished my second read-through of *Chapman,* I went out for an afternoon of sailing on a friend's boat, one that was similar in size to the boat our family was planning to purchase. I was able to try out many of the things I had read about: sail trim, upwind and downwind techniques, handling in close quarters, even knot tying. It was only by the grace of God that my friend didn't throw me overboard, as I repeatedly— and annoyingly—demonstrated my newly acquired book knowledge.

As we were headed back toward the marina in the late afternoon, my friend remarked that we might see his daughter out on the water. She and a friend had purchased a daysailer together and were planning to be out that day, so we began to scan the area, looking for their bright yellow hull.

> *Placing our faith in God will help us deal with every aspect of contemporary living, even the parts we never thought we would have to deal with.*

It wasn't long before we spotted it—upside down in the water. In a very short time, we dropped our sails, started the motor, hung the boarding ladder over the side, and prepared a throwing rope in case we might need it.

As we approached the capsized daysailer, we could see that the two young women were having trouble righting it—they could get the mast horizontal to the water, but they couldn't get it to come up any farther. They told us that they had been trying for more than half an hour, and it was obvious that they were getting very tired.

I called out to them, "Try this: One of you stand on the centerboard and put your hands on the rail; the other one get behind her on the centerboard and grab hold of the top straps of her life vest. Then both of you lean back as far as you can."

It took them a moment to get into the position I had described, but as soon as they did, and leaned back, the capsized boat popped back up to vertical. Unfortunately, it wasn't pointing into the wind, so it immediately went over again. But the young women quickly got the boat pointed in the right direction, tried the maneuver again—successfully, this time—and we towed them back to the marina.

Question: Was *Chapman* relevant to my sailing? Parts of it certainly were, as I expected they would be. But even the parts I never thought I would need to know proved helpful as my sailing brought me into contact with other boaters.

In the same way, if we substitute "Christianity" for *Chapman* and "life" for sailing, we can see that many parts of the Christian faith will be immediately relevant to our lives, while other parts may be relevant only at some future time. One of the amazing things about placing our faith in God is that God not only knows what we are worried about today, but also prepares us for what we will need to know down the road.

Take the Ten Commandments, for example. As a guide to daily living, they can't be beat. They are immediately applicable, easy to learn, and never out of date. The same is true of many of the stories of the Old Testament, and even many parts of the four gospels. They are easy to understand, the lessons are as relevant today as they ever were, and they will prove useful for our entire lives.

Now consider one of the biblical passages on marriage, such as chapter 5 of Paul's letter to the Ephesians or the third chapter of Colossians. If you are a single person, you might not think that these verses are relevant—but they could be someday. You may not be worrying about marriage right now, but the teaching on marriage will be there for you if and when that day comes.

Marriage is an easy example. It's not surprising that the Christian faith would have something to say about marriage. But what about more difficult contemporary issues, such as dealing with infertility, raising a blended family, identifying the role of women in the workplace, or even learning how to deal with overwhelming stress and responsibilities at work? Does our faith equip us for these challenges?

Let's see. There is no shortage of women in the Bible dealing with infertility (Hannah, Sarah, Rachel, Manoah, and Elizabeth come to mind). Jacob's family was as blended as could be—with many of the same issues blended families deal with today. The Bible offers many perspectives on the role of women—read the stories of Esther, Deborah, and Rahab, to name just a few. And as for managing a heavy work load, check out the story of how Moses' father-in-law, Jethro, taught him to delegate responsibility (Exodus 18).

I don't want to create the impression that the Bible is nothing more than a reference library—Have a problem? Look it up! Rather, I want to say that placing our faith in God will help us deal with every aspect of contemporary living, even the parts we never thought we would have to deal with.

As a sailor, I never thought I would have to know how to right a capsized daysailer. And as a Christian, there are many things in life that I can't anticipate needing to know. It gives me great comfort to realize that my faith in God is not only relevant for the things that concern me today, but that God is also preparing me for the things that I will need to know tomorrow.

Questions for reflection and discussion

1. What are some contemporary issues that concern you the most? Do you think the Bible might address these issues? Why or why not?

2. When we are students in school, why are we so often required to learn subjects (art history, music appreciation, calculus) that seem to have little or no relevance to the careers we have chosen?

3. How is it possible for a set of moral instructions like the Ten Commandments, written thousands of years ago, to still be relevant today?

4. God's Word has been translated onto audiotapes, video presentations, and even CD-ROMs. Worship has also taken on more contemporary forms. As long as the content is preserved, are these good ways to make the Christian faith more relevant?

5. *Chapman Piloting,* the "sailor's Bible," has gone through more than sixty-three editions since it was first published. Why hasn't the Bible been "updated" with regular revisions?

CHAPTER
12

"is it good enough just to be good enough?"

Do I have to go to church to get to heaven?

During a radio interview, Garrison Keillor, author and host of the program A Prairie Home Companion, *once remarked that going to church doesn't make someone a Christian any more than sleeping in the garage makes someone a car. I suspect that doesn't really come as a surprise to anyone. A car cannot become a car by being parked in the garage; it was already an automobile long before anyone drove it in there.*

We know where cars come from—well, sort of. I drive a Japanese car that was made in Ontario, Canada, and sold as a Geo through a Chevrolet dealer. At least we know for sure that every car started life in a factory somewhere—but where do Christians come from? If the church isn't an assembly line for believers, then where are the raw materials of humanity and faith brought together in such a way that the final product will be a follower of Jesus Christ?

For the answer to that question, we have to go back a little way in history—before the beginning of the world. The apostle Paul wrote, "Praise be to the God and Father of our Lord Jesus Christ, who has blessed us in the heavenly realms with every spiritual blessing in Christ. For he chose us in him before the creation of the world to be holy and blameless in his sight" (Ephesians 1:3-4).

To put that another way, we might say that God already had each one of us in mind before creating the world. Each of us was already a part of God's plan, and God already knew that it would be necessary for his Son, Jesus Christ, to be involved in the process of making us "holy and blameless," qualities that are necessary for anyone who wants to enter heaven (more about that in a moment).

> *If all of this seems to be exactly the opposite of the way things usually work in the world, then you have understood it correctly.*

From this planning and design stage, God moved into the manufacturing phase of creation, calling all things into being. The first couple of chapters of Genesis give us one perspective on how this occurred, which the author of Hebrews neatly summarizes by telling us, "By faith we understand that the universe was formed at God's command, so that what is seen was not made out of what was visible" (Hebrews 11:3). I'm not even going to pretend to understand how God could make something out of nothing. As one of my professors used to say, we simply "bow before the mystery" and accept it as a matter of faith.

If sin had not entered the world—in other words, if the world had remained perfect—God might have been able to simply enjoy creation, walking and talking with humanity, as with Adam and Eve in the Garden of Eden. But sin did enter in as the first couple chose to disobey God. In spite of this disobedience, God continued to love the world and remained actively involved in its development.

For example, King David, in Psalm 139, gives a beautiful account of how God was—and continues to be—active in the creation of every human being:

For you created my inmost being; you knit me together in my mother's womb. I praise you because I am fearfully and wonderfully made; your works are wonderful, I know that full well. My frame was not hidden from you when I was made in the secret place. When I was woven together in the depths of the earth, your eyes saw my unformed body. All the days ordained for me were written in your book before one of them came to be.

Although the language is poetic, the meaning is clear: God knew us before we were even born. God planned the course of our lives before we lived a single day. It would be as if Henry Ford could have mapped out the future course of every single Ford automobile before the first one ever rolled off the assembly line.

As we can see, then, the church is not what makes us Christians, but rather the place that helps us to discover what we were made to be. Going to church is not a prerequisite for going to heaven, but a place where we offer God our gratitude, praise, and service, *because* we believe that we are going to heaven.

This brings us back to that "holy and blameless" requirement I mentioned earlier. Sin and evil cannot enter heaven, so as Paul said, it is necessary for us to be made holy and blameless in God's sight.

Can we accomplish this by performing good works? Listen to the apostle Paul again: "For it is by grace you have been saved, through faith—and this not from yourselves, it is the gift of God—not by works, so that no one can boast. For we are God's workmanship, created in Christ Jesus to do good works, which God prepared in advance for us to do" (Ephesians 2:8-10).

Yes, we were made to do good works, but not in order to get us into heaven. That is God's work, through Jesus, which we receive by faith.

Let me put it another way. My car was manufactured in order to do good works (to get me where I need to go). When it breaks down (commits a sin), it can't fix itself by trying harder to drive me where I need to go. It needs to be repaired, something it simply can't do by itself. In the same way, trying harder to do good works cannot make any of us holy and blameless in God's sight. Only Jesus can "repair" our sinful condition—and he does this for us as a free gift, a gift of God's grace that we receive through faith, through believing that Jesus has given us this gift.

If all of this seems to be exactly the opposite of the way things usually work in the world, then you have understood it correctly. The normal way of gaining admission to a special place is to become a member of the club, so to speak, and work really hard until you've earned the right to enter the special place. But with the church, the simple act of attendance doesn't guarantee anything; neither does an impressive résumé of good works. Only faith in Jesus Christ, which God gives us as a free gift, guarantees our admission into God's eternal home.

You know, if simply going to church could make us into Christians, I might ask the Ferrari dealer if I could park my Geo in his garage overnight!

Questions for reflection and discussion

1. If going to church is an act of gratitude and praise in response to God's free gift of salvation, why do so many people worship with long faces?

2. Many people who do not believe in Jesus live exemplary lives. Why do you think so many of them are still unsatisfied? What are they missing?

3. If being a Christian were only about getting into heaven, would good works be necessary? What are some other reasons for being a Christian?

4. In what ways can you see that God has planned the course of your life? How does this make you feel about the future?

5. Why do you think God's way of providing salvation for people is so different from the world's way of doing things? Why does God give away salvation for free?

"what's the bottom line?"

What must I do to be saved?

I started this book by telling you how I used to stand at the side of my father's workbench, carefully observing him as he repaired watches and clocks. I didn't choose to become a horologist (that's the proper name for a watchmaker), but I came to understand enough about it that I was amazed at my father's wisdom and skill. Even more, I was amazed by his patience with me—a gift that grew out of his love.

Perhaps in reading this book, you have gained a greater appreciation for the wisdom and skill—and patience—of our heavenly Father. Although you may have more questions now than when you started reading (which is true for me too!) you may have seen enough of how our Father works to trust that his Word is true, and that God's loving will for you is always for your good.

Part of that will is for us to acknowledge Jesus Christ as our Savior. The apostle Paul wrote that God "wants all men to be saved and to come to a knowledge of the truth. For there is one God and one mediator between God and men, the man Christ Jesus, who gave himself as a ransom for all men" (1 Timothy 2:4-6). (God wants this for women too, of course; we have to remember the time in which Paul was writing.)

No special knowledge is required before someone can believe that Jesus Christ is the Lord—no secret handshake, no mysterious ritual, no precisely worded prayer. A simple yes to God's invitation to acknowledge Jesus as your Savior and Lord is all that's necessary.

If you are ready to say that yes to God's offer of salvation today, go ahead—I'll wait a moment until you're done talking to God. . . .

Did you do it? Did you say yes to God, acknowledging Jesus as the Lord of your life? If so, may I offer a prayer for you?

Dear Father, thank you for letting us stand along-side your workbench as we've thought about some hard questions together. Thank you for letting us see your wisdom and skill, and above all, your love. Thank you that your love was most fully revealed to us in your Son, Jesus Christ, who died to take away our sins.

Thank you, too, Father, for every person who has just said yes to your invitation to accept Jesus Christ as Savior and Lord. Guide each of these new believers to a fellowship of faith where they can keep asking questions, even as they offer you their worship and service in gratitude for your free gift.

Continue to surround us with your love, keeping our faith strong until that day when Jesus returns. May we await his return with joy and anticipation. In Jesus' name we pray. Amen.

"To him who is able to keep you from falling and to present you before his glorious presence without fault and with great joy—to the only God our Savior be glory, majesty, power and authority, through Jesus Christ our Lord, before all ages, now and forevermore! Amen" (Jude 24-25).